I0789183
COMMON SENSE 2.0:
MILITARY VETERANS' MANIFESTO
IN SUPPORT OF THE AMERICAN
PATRIOT DONALD J. TRUMP
AUTHORS ANONYMOUS

Copyright 2020: Free Veterans Movement

This is a political work of Opinion. The Authors' opinions are their own and do not necessarily reflect the opinions of the American Patriot Donald J. Trump, any member of his family, or any member of his Administration and should in no way be construed as such. Facts as given in this work have been interpreted by the authors' with their combined years of experience.

This work is being published anonymously to protect the authors from the likely blowback and possible reprisals from the Liberal threat to this great country.

All Rights Reserved. Portions of this work may be quoted without permission of the Authors or Publishers for the purposes of promotion via Social Media, websites, blogs, etcetera so long as attribution and a **sales link** are included with the quote.

Long Live the United States of America and Long Live the Great American Patriot Donald J. Trump.

If you found this work via any Social Media channel, such as but not limited to, Twitter, Facebook, Instagram or anywhere else, please note that whoever shared it may not necessarily endorse it.

We wholeheartedly encourage you to share this work and its sales links on your Social Media channels, tagging President Trump, members of his family and Administration, and any other American Patriot.

COMMON SENSE 2.0:

MILITARY VETERANS' MANIFESTO IN SUPPORT OF THE AMERICAN PATRIOT DONALD J. TRUMP

AUTHORS ANONYMOUS

PREFACE

The authors of this work wish to acknowledge first and foremost the sacrifices made by **Our Veterans**, the **American Patriots** who have served in our Armed Forces since the **Inception and Founding of our Great Nation**. It is because of their service and sacrifices that we, as a Nation, enjoy the freedoms and liberties that we do today. Without their sacrifice and service, we would not today be blessed with the Greatest World Leader America has ever known—**DONALD J. TRUMP**.

Is Donald J. Trump perfect? In a simple word—YES. He is Exactly the Leader this Country **NEEDED** in the disastrous aftermath of Barrack Hussein Obama, a.k.a. Barry Soetoro. This Manifesto isn't about Backwards Barry, though. Real Americans know the damage the Beltway Bumbler caused, not just in our own land, but all around the whole world. It would suffice to say that Barack Hussein Obama was the worst President we have ever had since Herbert Hoover and the most divisive incompetent since James Buchanan. To anyone with historical sense, knowledge, and a passion for **Keeping America Great**, this is **Common Sense**. To the Misguided Media and the Liberal Left who infect our nation with their lies, Hussein Obama might as well be the second coming of Lincoln.

This Manifesto is a direct challenge to the Liberal Left who so ardently try to besmirch Our President. **We see you**, **Loser Lefties**. We know your garbage tactics. You will not win. You cannot win, because you cannot suppress the **Truth** from **True American Patriots**, no matter how hard you try to spin it. Your fictional world will eventually come crashing down around you as it always, without fail, does. Your true colors will be revealed for all to see, and your hypocrisy and blatant **Anti-Americanism** will be on display and you will be judged accordingly, not only in the eyes of your Fellow Americans, but also in the eyes of God come Judgment Day.

This Manifesto is a presentation of the important facts as we see them, and as every Good, Patriotic American should see them. The Truth will always come out. We hope to shine a light on this Truth, and give hope to every American Patriot that our Great Nation will continue to flourish with another 4 years for President Donald J. Trump as our leader.

The authors don't hope to convert anyone here, only to enlighten and give Hope and Faith to those who support the American Patriot Donald J. Trump. Should someone read this and come to their senses, then we will have done our job far better than we anticipated.

To the Good and True Patriots reading this Manifesto: we thank you for your support. Without **YOU**, none of this would matter. Without your undying and unwavering Patriotic Spirit, all would be lost. Keep the Faith, Patriots.

Be in Good Health and in Good Cheer for:

YOU ARE NOT ALONE. WE STAND UNITED WITH YOU IN OUR VOCAL, UNEQUIVOCAL, AND ABSOLUTE SUPPORT OF THE GREAT AMERICAN PATRIOT PRESIDENT DONALD J. TRUMP.

INTRODUCTION

There are four principal authors of this Manifesto, each with their own unique insights and perspective into the Presidency and the State of the Nation as it is today under the leadership of President Donald J. Trump.

In concert, these four authors have penned this Manifesto, which you will read first, directly after this Introduction. The Authors chose not to write separately, but together as a full display of the Unity and Accord they feel regarding the material and opinions presented.

As is stated on the Copyright page, their identities are being shielded as they fear reprisals from the Left. Although no longer on Active Duty service, each author feels strongly that their Life and Liberty could very well be at stake should their identities be revealed. Details of their individual service shall not be forthcoming (at this time) for that reason alone. It's a sad state of affairs that these Patriots need to remain anonymous, but they are willing to risk all the things they have collectively fought and served for in order to publish this most important work. They feel it is **imperative** these thoughts and ideas be presented to the world in support of President Donald J.

Trump.

An independent third-party is responsible for compiling and producing this manifesto, under the guidance of the four principal authors. This third party is also remaining anonymous in order to avoid the same sort of reprisals. As you very well know, Liberals have a truly nasty habit of crucifying anyone who proclaims a different world view, particularly one based in truth, not fiction. Everyone involved in the production and publication of this book is a true American Patriot, and is Proud to bring this work into the world for you.

Though not necessarily reminiscent of Thomas Paine's *Common Sense* pamphlet written in 1775 – 1776, the authors have chosen to draw inspiration from this and as such chose the befitting title **Common Sense 2.0** to convey their important thoughts and observations, their informed opinions.

Unfortunately for the State of the Union, there is a rather large segment of the population of the U.S. today that lacks the good common sense to realize a competent leader when they see one. We have seen time and time again in the contradictory Liberal Media how President Donald J. Trump's words are twisted and misquoted, how they are wholly misrepresented to make him look bad, not only here at home, but abroad, as well. The Liberal Media would have you believe President Trump is the Devil in disguise. But we know better, and if you're reading this, you do, too.

At the end of this book you will find **multiple pages** of **ACCOMPLISHMENTS** that the Great American Patriot Donald J. Trump has had since becoming the Greatest President in American History. Facts are facts, folks. He's done more for this country than any other president **EVER**. It cannot be denied. Halfwit Hucksters and Petty Pundits can argue until they are blue in the face to the contrary, but the proof of the truth is far too obvious to anyone willing to simply open their eyes and see it. It's not necessary to actually like President Trump, but it is necessary to acknowledge his triumphs as leader of the Greatest Country in the world.

The Authors wish to express to you, the reader, that your Support of this work and of the President inspires in them a sense of faith that all is not lost in America. We as a nation have teetered dangerously close to the edge of oblivion and have been brought back from the brink of destruction into a new age of Growth and Prosperity thanks to the Great American Patriot Donald J. Trump. By Supporting this work and others like it, you are enabling the real **TRUTH** of what's happening in America today to be brought forth for the entire world to see.

Profits from this Work will go towards Supporting and Furthering the causes that are nearest and dearest to our President, Donald J. Trump. In essence, the money you spent on this book will be used to continue to Make America Great today, in the here and now, and forevermore.

Please do consider additional donations to our **Free Veterans Movement** in order that we may continue to publish and bring to you and to the world the Truth and the Way. Consider purchasing additional copies of this work for friends and family; Share it on **ALL** of your social media channels (**Twitter**, **Instagram**, **Facebook**, etc...), being sure to tag President Trump, his family, his Administration, and his Supporters so that they, too, can help us get this Urgent Message to the world. Tag also your Local and National Representatives in your posts.

And lastly...**POST OFTEN!!!** The Liberal threats to this country **DO NOT TAKE BREAKS** from spreading their hate-filled messages of deceit, and **WE MUST NOT FALTER IN COUNTERACTING THIS EVIL!!!**

We, as a United Group of Patriots, **MUST** act to counter the Propaganda the Left inundates our news feeds with. It's our **Duty** as **American Patriots**.

We **MUST** protect the Integrity of Our Nation and the Office of The President of The United States of America.

Our very **SURVIVAL** is at stake, Patriots. Surely you see this as clearly as we do.

The Great American Patriot Donald J. Trump needs Our **CONTINUAL SUPPORT!** Do not waver in the face of Opposition, Patriots. Do not waver in your Convictions and Beliefs.

UNITED WE STAND; DIVIDED WE FALL.

And we'll tell you right here and now, Patriots: **WE. WILL. NOT. FALL.**

We **WILL NOT** give in to the Tyranny of the Radical Left who wants to disarm us and render the Second Amendment NULL AND VOID, leaving us defenseless against Evil and Injustice.

We **WILL NOT** let Liberal Commies take God and the Church from our very Homes and our Schools.

We **WILL NOT** let our Children be Indoctrinated and Endangered by Deceptive Democrats hell-bent on destroying what we Good, God-Fearing Americans have worked so hard to accomplish.

Stand Strong and Proud, Patriots, for you live in the Greatest Country in the World. You represent and are represented by the Greatest Leader of our times. With your help, we will usher President Trump into 4 More Years of Leadership, Growth, and Success!

What's At Stake?

This may seem like a question with an obvious answer, and for the most part it is—if you've been paying attention and not living under a rock for the past dozen years or so.

The importance of leadership in this country hasn't always been a clear concept, or so it seems to us. In years past, particularly in the run up to election years, many candidates have made fanciful promise after fanciful promise in an effort to get elected. And what happens once they do get elected? Those promises fly straight out the White House window, only to drown and disappear in the quagmire of The Swamp that is Washington D.C.

Political games and maneuvering like this are so much the norm, that when President Trump made the decision to run for office many people didn't take him seriously. They discounted virtually everything that he said right out of the gate, without as much as a second thought. But, *why*? He was saying and promising things that many people wanted to hear and believe. He was speaking to the hopes and dreams of millions of Americans, just like you and me, Patriot.

We'll tell you why: it's because he was speaking

truths that those on the Left didn't want **YOU** to hear, and they spared **NO EXPENSE** attempting to make sure you were kept in the dark, blinded as to President Trump's true intentions.

We heard a lot about "locker room" talk, about President Trump being too brash and crude, et-cetera. That's BS and we all know it. The President was attacked then and continues to be attacked to this day for **speaking his mind** and not pandering to the malleable masses. He speaks like a Man's Man, not like a Pandering Politician. And because of this, his messages were—and still are—often misinter-preted and misquoted by his opponents.

He was speaking truth about immigration and how it continually degrades American Society in ways we are still trying to fathom and come to terms with, and likely will be for several generations to come, even after slowing the flow into the country. Now, do we think that immigration into the country by foreign nationals should stop altogether? No, we don't.

However, we think that **ONLY** those individuals who have something of **SUBSTANTIVE** value to add to our society should be allowed to move here and integrate. Doctors, Scientists, Engineers: people who add true value to the nation as a whole, and who can live up to the **Core Values** we hold as a country. We'll speak more on this very important topic later in the book.

President Trump was speaking truth about getting the United States **OUT** of the Middle East. He said our Troops didn't belong there, and we agreed with him wholeheartedly. He kept his promise about drawing down the number of Troops that are in harm's way in regions that don't want us there. As a result, we see more and more peaceful resolutions to conflict happening in the region. President Donald J. Trump is responsible for that, no one else.

President Trump was speaking truth about abolishing and repealing Obamacare, the disastrous and very often harmful directives and policies put into place by the Oblivious Obama administration that **FORCED** American citizens to buy insurance they didn't want or need; if they didn't buy this crappy insurance they were made to pay a **FINE**, which to our minds amounts to government mandated **EXTORTION**, plain and simple.

And these so-called "insurance plans" came at costs that were so outrageously exorbitant that they left many American families in the utterly reprehensible situation of being broke, broken, and ultimately without the proper and adequate healthcare coverage they needed for themselves and their loved ones to survive even the simplest of illnesses or injuries.

President Donald J. Trump restored the **CHOICE** of Healthcare Coverage to every American Family. For that service to the nation alone he should be nominated for and receive a **Nobel Peace Prize**—but Liberals will never allow that to happen.

President Trump was speaking truth about America First, a concept so foreign to the Liberal Left that it quite literally scared them shitless. Liberals could see their lives of endless easy wealth and riches vanishing and drying up before their very eyes, all because President Trump wanted to bring jobs and industry back home to America, where they belong.

Why do you think Democrats were so against bringing wealth back into the United States as opposed to keeping it across borders and overseas?

Their bank accounts.

Plain and simple greed.

Keeping production and manufacturing outside of the United States allows these corporate giants —whose teats Democrats suckle at with such extreme avarice twenty-four hours a day, seven days a week, fifty-two weeks a year—to reap HUGE profits while avoiding paying their fair share of taxes. The Globalist Elite under the sway of George Soros and his legions want to keep filling their pockets while keeping the American working class pinned helplessly underneath their collectivist boot. They will keep real Americans down, and give a few ill-gotten crumbs to the crooks and the charlatans who wreck our country as we speak.

How Un-American is that???

In line with this thought, President Trump spoke of 'draining The Swamp' in D.C. and that really, *really* shook up Democrats, so much so that they stopped at nothing to try to prevent his **lawful** election to the Presidency. They even went so far as to concoct vicious lies and blatant falsehoods accusing Russia of meddling in the election in favor of President Donald J. Trump.

We'll say this about those baseless accusations: even if it were true that Russia or China or any other sovereign nation somehow managed to interfere in the 2016 presidential election, we should be thanking them for giving us the best leader we've ever had.

To be perfectly clear here, **WE DO NOT** believe that any other nation played any part, in any way whatsoever, in the election of Donald J. Trump to the Office of the President of the United States of America. All-American Patriots like you and us are responsible for President Trump's election.

The countless investigations and queries into the matter—each one a **HUGE** waste of taxpayer money —have borne out this fact over and over again, yet Democrats and those with a Liberal Left agenda continue to make claims that they can neither back up nor provide proof for.

And this, Patriot, is the **ULTIMATE PROOF** of the plot against America by those who claim to be Patriotic Americans themselves. It's Shameful, Disgraceful, and utterly **TREASONOUS**.

Maybe you're beginning to get an inkling of what's at stake here. Our very **Freedom** and **Way of Life**, that's what.

If Democrats and the Liberal Left have their way with you, Patriot, the country you now know and love will cease to exist. It will no longer be the **Home of the Brave** or the **Land of the Free**.

It will morph into the **Home of the Oppressed**, the **Land of the Downtrodden**. A land where **Immigrants** and **Outsiders** have more rights than you, a **Native-Born American Citizen**. A place where good and honest Americans like us will see everything we've worked so hard for our whole lives stripped away and given to those who've done nothing to earn it other than sneak into the country. A place where Socialism has replaced the sacred **Constitution of the United States of America**.

Let us give you a glimpse of the future and the future of your children if President Donald J. Trump does not prevail.

- You'll work the same number of hours, but bring home half of the pay.
- Every state will become California—a PC police state where the criminals have the guns, your children will be given propa-

ganda instead of a proper education, and where white males are to be blamed for literally everything that has every happened in the history of the country.

- Rich celebrities who hide their wealth overseas will lecture you about how you need to give more to the State to help out the less fortunate—the less fortunate, you realize, are not working nearly as hard as yourself (if at all).

- You won't be safe in your own home, and you will need to constantly mentally prepare yourself for the day when you're burglarized, then sued by the burglar within the same week after they stub their toe on the way out while carrying your television.

- China will be a superpower and America will be like the U.K., a pathetic welfare state with no social mobility whose only export will be television and only import, curious tourists.

We simply cannot let that happen. Our Children and our Children's Children deserve so much better than that. We didn't serve our country for a collective term of nearly 100 years to stand by and allow Liberal Losers to make a mockery of all that this Proud Country stands for. What about the boys who died at Lexington and Concord, at Gettysburg, at

Normandy—did they suffer and make the ultimate sacrifice in order to let BLM and Antifa take over the streets and bully people believing in the American Way? **HELL NO, PATRIOT!**

We know, too, that you feel the same way and that you will step up and do what's right to preserve and protect our Great Nation against these clear and present dangers facing each and every one of us.

Your support isn't just wanted, it is **ABSOLUTELY VITAL**. If we are to defeat the nefarious forces that have aligned against us, we must all participate in protecting the Nation. Now is not the time in history to sit idly by. You do so at your own peril, and at the peril of our homeland. It is one minute to Midnight and the hour has never been darker. You might say that things were worse during the darkest hours of World War Two. You would be **wrong**. The difference is that the threat comes from inside our country. The threat comes from people masquerading as our own countrymen. It is an invisible enemy who is organized, calculating, and determined to destroy all that we hold most precious and dear.

We're not saying you have to go out to rallies every day or give political speeches from your front porch. We understand that not everyone can do those things, and **THAT'S OKAY**.

What we **ARE** saying is that you **SHOULD** make your voice heard via your Social Media channels. In today's world, there's no easier way to make your position known than on **Twitter** or **Facebook** or **Instagram** or any of the other powerful Social Media channels available. We don't want to keep repeating ourselves here, but we have to in order to make sure that the message is clear: **USING YOUR SOCIAL MEDIA CHANNELS TO SUPPORT PRESIDENT DONALD J. TRUMP IS ABSOLUTELY VITAL TO AMERICA!**

Share this book and others like it. Give it as a gift. Send it to a Liberal to piss them off. Send it to your Local AND National Representatives. Send a copy to your local News Media (print newspapers and magazines, television and radio stations, and online publications). The more you can spread the word, and the more copies you put of this work into the world, the better the chances we have of reaching people and instilling in them the importance of keeping Donald J. Trump as the President of the United States of America. It's a life or death situation, Patriot. We're counting on you. The Nation is counting on you.

PRESIDENT DONALD J. TRUMP IS COUNTING ON YOU!

IMMIGRATION NATION: HOW DID THE UNITED STATES BECOME THE ONE-STOP SHOP FOR IMMIGRANTS?

Fundamentally, as we stated earlier, we're not completely against immigration so long as it is strictly controlled immigration, and not the free-for-all horror show we've seen over the past decades. Now, of course, when we say that, we're talking about **legal** immigration.

When it comes to **illegal** immigration, we draw a hard line at the border. **The bottom line is this**: if you come into the United States illegally, without even bothering with the proper channels, then you **DO NOT BELONG HERE.** And as such, you should expect to be removed from our soil by whatever means necessary, including physical force. If you cannot respect the Law of the Land, then how can you expect the respect and protection of the Law as provided to legal citizens? ***

For too many years Liberal policies and laws allowed for immigrants to remain here once they set foot here. That's wrongheaded on so many levels. That's just like saying to your neighbor or to someone you don't even know: Well, I found my way to your yard and now I'm going to live here and take food from your refrigerator and money from your bank account and there's nothing you can do about it.

How is that even right by *any* stretch of the imagination? If you said it isn't, you're absolutely correct.

The argument always, without fail, bounces back to the topic of these immigrants aren't safe in their own countries. How and why should that be the problem of the American People? In case you haven't noticed, there are millions of us who don't feel safe in *our* own country these days, but you don't see us running away to some other place, trying to hop in for a free ride. We tough it out, do what we have to do to survive, and get on with it. That's the **very definition** of the American Way, Patriot.

President Trump understands this concept very clearly, which is why his stance on immigration is so focused and so intense. If every person in the world who was living in a dangerous or disadvantaged situation decided to up and come to the United States, what do you think would happen to all of us already here?

Where would *we* go?

What would *we* do?

How would *we* survive?

For too long Liberals have let the borders of the United States act as revolving doors for anybody and everybody who wanted to come here and set up shop, and more often than not, freeload off of the state and government for handouts so they could have tons of kids—many of who won't even bother to learn English. And what do those kids do? Turn around and have even more kids, perpetuating this cycle of freeloading off of the American Taxpayer, which is **YOU** and **ME**, Patriot.

We've seen the crime statistics, the welfare statistics. You've seen them, too. The money being spent on welfare for freeloading illegals alone would provide more than enough to improve education and healthcare programs for low-income Americans. You factor in the amount of money spent on criminal justice for illegals in this country, and it would blow your mind.

The United States has nearly twenty percent of the world's migrants. That number should blow your mind. And the reason they all come here? Up until recently, they knew they would have a practically free ride. President Trump promised he would change that, and it's just one of the promises he made during his campaign that he's kept. It's tougher than ever for immigrants to enter the country, and as well it should be. By this virtue alone, President Trump has made the Nation **better** and **stronger**.

Now we come to the subject of the United States Immigration and Customs Enforcement, better known as ICE. Democrats want to abolish ICE altogether, leaving the country vulnerable to unchecked illegal immigration. Just one more way Democrats are trying to destroy our country and us.

ICE serves one of the most important functions in our country today, in conjunction with the Department of Homeland Security. They investigate, find, and round up illegal immigrants and send them back to where they came from.

How anyone could even propose cuts to funding for this important work is beyond us. It's the very definition of **UN-AMERCIAN**.

On the contrary, we call for an increase in funding for ICE as well as United States Border Patrol and for the Department of Homeland Security as a whole.

What could be more important to an American Citizen than the protection of our homeland and our borders? As far as we're concerned, this should be a top priority, and with the Trump Administration, it is. Democrats fight President Trump tooth and nail on it, but he steadfastly refuses to give up on protecting our country. He's doing his job and doing it well in this regard. Don't dare believe any BS you hear otherwise.

What other disastrous past administrations have done to weaken our immigration laws, President Trump, his Cabinet, and his Advisors have worked tirelessly to put right and to strengthen. He's done these things because he cares about our country in a way that not many other presidents have. The Media have truly punished him for it, too, accusing him of such things as 'putting kids in cages' and keeping families apart. But President Trump takes these criticisms in stride and continues on day-by-day, doing the right things for America.

Legal Immigration isn't bad, when it goes through the proper system of checks and balances. Illegal Immigration is one of the worst problems in the country today. Without the hard work of President Trump and his team, the country would have been overrun from our southern borders by now; that's a **fact**. These are facts that Liberals don't want to share with you, but they are facts nonetheless that are so very easily verifiable. Democrats' denial of the obvious would be almost humorous if it weren't for the potentially deadly consequences involved for our country.

Support for the Department of Homeland Security, ICE, and US Border Patrol must continue undiminished if we, as a nation, are to continue to live lives of freedom and prosperity.

If we are to guarantee the safety and security of our families, Patriot, we **MUST** see to it that Donald J.

Trump is elected to a second term. We must not lose the progress his administration has made by seeing a Dangerous Democrat take office again. The consequences would be very dire indeed were that to happen.

We know we can count on you, Patriot, to spread the word and make known your thoughts and feelings to the world. Your support of this book is **ABSOLUTE PROOF** of your commitment to America and keeping America Safe and Protected from all threats, both from outside our borders and within them.

*** **Please note that we DO NOT advocate violence against illegals or suspected illegals by private citizens.** If you suspect there may be illegal activity in your area, immediately call **1-866-347-2423** to report suspicious criminal activity to the **U.S. Immigration and Customs Enforcement (ICE) Homeland Security Investigations (HSI) Tip Line** 24 hours a day, 7 days a week, every day of the year.

It's important that you let the trained professionals handle situations like that. This is not only for your safety and protection, but to ensure that any illegals have no legal recourse against you which might allow them to find a loophole in the law and stay in the country. We know you don't want that to happen, Patriot. You know as well as we do that there are legions of Liberal Lawyers lined up to try to protect illegals in this country. **Don't give them the ammunition they need to undermine our society. It's not worth it, Patriot. Let ICE do the job.**

PRESIDENT TRUMP'S COVID-19 RESPONSE

You've very likely seen in the news lately reports disparaging President Trump's response to the COVID-19, or coronavirus, pandemic that's gripped the world since early in the year. This is a shining example of how the Liberal Left Media twists and misrepresents his words and portrays his intentions as no good for the American People.

We would argue that the President's response has been totally in line with many other world leaders' positions, particularly our allies. The President relies on those around him to provide him with the most accurate and up-to-date information on myriad topics each and every day. He takes this information into account, and with input from his Advisors and in conjunction with the proper authorities, makes decisions that are for the good of every person in the country. This is as it should be in a fair and just society.

We believe that President Trump may have been undermined by those around him who wished to see him disparaged, mocked, torn down. While we have no direct proof of this ourselves, it's pretty clear when you follow the events leading up to where we are today (at the time of this publication).

The very fact that President Trump stated he didn't want to cause a panic by declaring a national emergency or some such thing is direct proof, in our eyes, that he had the best interests of the American People at heart. What good would have come from creating panic? No good whatsoever, that we can tell you. Many more would have died as a result. We truly believe that, Patriot.

All of the information publicly available about the virus during the early stages of the pandemic suggested that, while some preventative measures could be taken, there was no guarantee that it could be stopped or even slowed down. Information that has since come out can be both hard to understand and at times blatantly misleading. Certain officials in the government who were or are in charge of ascertaining, verifying, and disseminating that information haven't done a very good job of it. **Let's be perfectly frank here: they've done a piss poor job of it.** These individuals' poor performance has had the unfortunate effect of making or seeming to make President Trump look bad as far as his response to the pandemic. This fact goes back to our earlier point of certain people surrounding President Trump attempting, and in some cases succeeding, in undermining him. Not only is this **treasonous**, it has needlessly cost American lives.

All that said the bottom line truth of this pandemic matter is this: it falls to the responsibility of state governors to ensure the protection of citizens in their respective states. Each state is equipped to respond to emergency situations just like these, with some assistance from the Federal Government, and many Blue states simply were not prepared. Who knows where theses States' Crisis Response funding went? We don't know, but we can speculate and you surely can, too, Patriot. It can't be said that President Trump is responsible for States' failures. You just can't do it. We would like to see a full accounting of States' Crisis Response spending prior to, during, and after this pandemic. Then perhaps we can determine who the real culprits or villains are in this situation.

Many of these governors—nearly all Democrats where the biggest outbreaks occurred, by the way; no big surprise there—didn't step up to the plate to take the necessary precautions to protect their citizens. When their inaction began causing havoc in their states, they turned the blame to President Trump. This, as we now know and understand, was wholly unfair. These loser Democrat governors must step up and accept the responsibility for their states, whether it be publicly or through the court systems, meaning prosecution for negligence—and maybe even embezzlement if it's determined that their Crisis Response budgets were raided for frivolous stuff.

President Trump has done plenty for the country

during this emergency, from fast-tracking numerous vaccine development programs to see that Americans are protected as soon as possible, to orchestrating deals with PPE (person protective equipment) manufacturers and medical equipment manufacturers and suppliers, both in the United States and abroad. President Trump cleared the way for and quickly signed several stimulus packages that have helped both American Citizens and American Businesses. At the time of this writing, Democrats were holding up an additional stimulus package that would provide American families with additional funds to ensure that they can continue to survive while the economy bounces back and domestic spending increases.

No other world leader has taken the steps to adopt measures that President Trump has, and those that have come close didn't do so with nearly the speed or efficiency he has. If Democrats hadn't stood in his way, Emergency Relief would have made it to American Families even sooner.

We firmly believe that no other president could have done the job better than President Trump; certainly not a Democrat. It's no secret that Democrats don't care at all for people or their health. Just look at their track records when it comes to voting for healthcare related laws. It speaks for itself. It is utterly **unconscionable** that Democrats would hold up a stimulus package simply because it doesn't include Pork Barrel spending for their cronies and special interests. It's just further proof that **Democrats hate America**. That's right, Patriot. **DEMOCRATS HATE YOU AND YOUR FAMILY. THEY DON'T CARE WHETHER YOU LIVE OR DIE. THEY'VE PROVEN THAT TIME AND TIME AGAIN WITH THEIR ACTIONS AND INACTIONS.**

Was President Trump's COVID-19 response perfect? Maybe not, but he was working as hard as he could with the information that was made available to him, all while surrounded by multiple factions who wished to see him fail. Not only did they wish to see him fail, **they actively worked at trying to make that a reality.** There's no disputing that. Just look at the volume of turnover in his Cabinet. All of those who have been fired have proven to be disloyal, and that disloyalty led to direct and persistent threats against the country. These traitorous insiders, coupled with the venomous Liberal Media, have tried to tear down President Trump from Day One. That's another unarguable **FACT**.

But still President Trump has persevered, continuing to do what he believes to be right for the American People—people just like you and me, Patriot—every single day. No matter the backlash that comes his way, no matter how evilly the Media portrays him and twists his words, he has remained steadfast in his Loyalty and Patriotism to the United States of America, and every single citizen within our borders.

Without fail, our President has stood his ground against factions that would have forced a lesser man to capitulate to Un-American ethics. President Donald J. Trump **LOVES** America and his COVID-19 response is full proof of that unassailable fact.

The country and the world have a long way to go still in the fight against COVID-19. With President Donald J. Trump leading the way, the United States of America will once again show the world what American Superiority means. You can count on that, Patriot.

We know you'll do your part in the fight against Democrat Tyranny, just like the **Great American Patriot Donald J. Trump**.

PRESIDENT TRUMP AND THE AMERICAN TROOPS: A COMMANDER-IN-CHIEF FOR THE AGES

One of President Donald J. Trump's very early campaign promises was to bring home US Troops who were stationed overseas in areas where, in his estimation, they didn't belong or need to be, fighting in wars that should never have been waged in the first place.

The big area of concern when it comes to our Troops has to be the Middle East. We know that you'll agree with us, Patriot, when we say with raised voices that **our Troops do not belong in the desert** where they are subject to bodily harm by insurgents and Islamic Terrorists who have no respect at all for Human life, and most especially for the American Way of Life which our Soldiers represent.

We spent our fair share of time deployed to places like **Iraq** and **Afghanistan** so we speak with absolute authority on the matter. Quite literally **NO ONE** wanted us there. We were constantly surrounded by threats to our safety and our very lives. We each lost soldiers and friends to IEDs (improvised explosive devices) planted by Islamic terrorists for the express and sole purpose of killing or maiming US Soldiers and contractors.

But you don't have to take our word for it, Patriot. Head on over to your nearest V.F.W. Post and talk to some of your local Veteran Heroes who spent time in the 'sandbox' as we call it. But do so only if you have a strong stomach because you'll likely hear stories that are straight out of a horror movie—but they will be **true**.

So many of our young Men and Women who just wanted to serve their Country lost their lives to terrorists and insurgents, and for what? So some slick, fancy politician could line his pockets and fill his bank accounts with kickbacks from Special Interest Groups. **It is absolutely vile and sickening.**

Every red cent those corrupt bastards took over the course of the Wars that have been waged in the name of 'Democracy' are indeed RED with the blood of our innocent soldiers who were only following orders. Every Widow or Widower made, every Child that lost a mother or father or brother or sister, every life lost to those impossible-to-win wars, every life *affected*—that misery and sadness and heartbreak is on the hands of Warmongering political **Traitors** who wouldn't dare let their Son or Daughter, Brother or Sister or anyone close to them fight.

President Donald J. Trump promised to end that needless bloodshed and he has kept his promise to the best of his ability. We have fewer Troops in the region now than when he took office, and every month the Trump Administration explores more ways to bring our young Men and Women back home, where they belong. In no way would this have happened under Hillary Clinton and her people. In fact, we could make an honest bet that Hillary, insecure, beholden to globalist interests, would probably escalate the warfare in the region in order to prove "how tough" she is dealing with the terrorists.

In addition to Troop Withdrawals in the region, President Trump has worked tirelessly to broker **Peace Talks** with Middle Eastern governments and militant groups like the Taliban in order to further lessen the need for a United States military presence in the region.

We neither approve of nor condone interaction with groups like the Taliban, but we see the wisdom in brokering these types of engagements as they can and will lead to peace in the region. Peace anywhere around the world is a good thing for everyone, but for our Troops especially as they are the ones who are sacrificed when there is perpetual war like we've seen in the Middle East for decades now.

We wholeheartedly and without reservation commend President Donald J. Trump for his massive, tireless efforts in this regard. Virtually no other

American president in history has made the kind of inroads into a lasting peace process like he has. Again, more facts that Dangerous Democrats would rather you not know or ignore. Well, Patriot, we refuse to ignore the facts and we know you do, too.

CREATION OF THE UNITED STATES SPACE FORCE

At the direction of President Trump, the U.S. Space Force (USSF) is a brand new branch of the United States Armed Forces which was established on December 20, 2019, with the official enactment of the Fiscal Year 2020 National Defense Authorization Act. The USSF will be stood-up over the following 18 months.

The USSF was established within the Department of the Air Force, which means that the Secretary of the Air Force has overall responsibility for the USSF, under the guidance and direction of the Secretary of Defense and the President of the United States. Additionally, a four-star general known as the Chief of Space Operations (CSO) will serve as the senior military member of the USSF.

The USSF is the military branch that will organize, train, and equip United States space forces in order to protect American and Allied interests in space. It will also ultimately serve to provide space capabilities to the joint forces. USSF responsibilities will include developing military space professionals capable of performing duties in the rigors of space, acquisition of necessary military space systems (to include planetary Defensive capabilities), maturing current military doctrine for space power and prowess, and organizing space forces to present to Combatant Commands.

There was much laughter and mockery when USSF was initially announced. Many Left-leaning pundits jumped all over it as though it was a joke. Patriot, we can assure that the USSF is **no joke**.

As we and other nations continue to explore space, both in the proximity of Earth and well beyond, we are subject to the absolute unknown. We have to be prepared for whatever lies ahead on this path of continued exploration.

President Trump had the foresight to create the USSF in order that we as a Nation are protected from threats that are as-yet unknown. In truth, creation of this type of military service should have been started the moment we set foot on the moon.

The fact of the matter that China is looking to expand its Empire to the Stars should be of no surprising revelation. The Chinese have been consistent in their attempts to steal our technology and to make the Moon their first colony. China, with its intrigues, manipulations, useful idiots, and hacks, have stolen decades of data and research to make this concept a frightening reality.

It will be no real surprise whatsoever to hear in the next few years of a Chinese manned space launch, a new Chinese rocket, a new Chinese probe, a new Chinese satellite. And do you think for one moment that they are **NOT** planning on using their "research" for nefarious military purposes? Hell NO!

The Chinese are doing one of the fastest military buildups in world history, on nearly the same level as the sort of pre-War buildup that was occurring in Hitler's Germany. The billions of dollars they are spending (billions that could be used to help their own people, mind you) on defense and space research is to make sure that they, not the USA, will be the top dog when it comes to military might. They are prepping for a world where the U.S. asks permission to move its bowels, let alone work towards defending its own interests.

President Trump has been smart enough to put together yet another agency that will combat the threat of the Chinese in space and ensure that we have peaceful access to the solar system and the universe and not have to live in a world where the Chinese can drop nuclear weapons on us as if they were throwing rocks from a freeway overpass at oncoming traffic.

The Liberal Left of course loves to mock the idea and even invested money in a television program that no one watches in order to take another jab at our President, but when our children can look up to an American moon and feel free of any fear that the other side could dominate us from Space, we know that they will always be thanking Donald J. Trump for showing initiative instead of spinelessness.

Who knows, in a few decades, the first monument on the moon will probably be Donald J. Trump's face, carved into the side of a lunar mountain range —a new Mt. Rushmore, and a testament to President Donald J. Trump's lasting Great American Legacy.

FIGHTING THE MARXIST THREAT: PRESIDENT TRUMP VERSUS THE COMMUNISTS

Americans of all backgrounds and persuasions are sick of the Marxist assault on our Constitutional Values. And the threat is something that we've seen up close and personal with classrooms around the country turned into virtual **Indoctrination Centers**. We see it with the constant bombardment of puerile propaganda that floods every baseball, basketball, and football stadium with these loads of losers who are spoiled from the first moment they get on the field who 'take a knee' against the American system.

The same 'awful' system, mind you, that is making sure that every one of these grunting creeps who play games for a living can go back home to their mansions and their exotic girlfriends without one moment thinking about the common man scraping by from Detroit to El Paso.

The same system that allows them to make money doing what they love—which certainly wouldn't be the case in Communist Cuba or China.

In Cuba they'd be lucky to make five dollars a day playing baseball in Havana. In Miami playing professional ball? Well, Patriot, you fill in the blank.

Who are these people to lecture us? America has had some major faults over the years but what country hasn't? The British with their monarchy and their nonsensical parliament that we broke away from; is that something we should change our system to? The French, where every election 25 percent of the population votes for a Soviet style dictatorship? Or Germany?

The moment America decides to either legitimatize socialism, invade other countries in order to gain resources, or allow the disgusting Marxist-Leninist threat to actually run for office, that's the moment that America will commit spiritual suicide. And believe you me, Patriot, that threat is certainly closer than it appears.

We see this in our TV shows as well that have to input some sort of snarky social justice commentary in even the most basic, simple sitcom situations, or our smart-mouth late night hosts who have such a "clever" thing to say about the main man in charge who actually had the guts to take the reins of power instead of sitting in an air-conditioned studio so outside of reality that it might as well be that they were doing their show from the Land of Oz.

Remember, President Trump actually worked as

a host of his own highly rated television show, **The Apprentice**. But unlike these other sniveling, simpering liberal lackeys out there, he actually **stood up** and decided to fight for us, the Real Americans. Not to just fight for higher ratings amongst the few Limousine Liberals still awake on the West Coast.

Kennedy, Eisenhower, and Truman would be quaking with rage if they saw the sort of people who are coming out of the woodwork to burn our Flags and our Businesses to the ground. They would wonder where the FBI was and why it wasn't crushing this red menace—but unfortunately theirs was the FBI of J. Edgar Hoover, not the FBI of James Clinton Comey.

They would be astounded at how far criminal lawlessness has come, brought forth and ushered in by violent and irrepressible Marxists who somehow survived the fall of the Soviet Union. Like cockroaches leaving a collapsed building, they go into the one next door, ready to infest every square inch of the place. The Left has lost its collective mind today, but let it be known that this has been a long time in the making.

Ever since the 1960s the United States, due to a consistent pattern of simpering kindness and open mindedness in our schools, started to produce one generation after another who were secretly taught that the United States is the center of evil. **The** words **genocide** and **slavery** have been used and abused to the point of nonsensicalness.

Every job working for a living is slavery; every government action that includes a member of the minority community is an act of genocide. The ethics of hard work have been replaced with the ethics of social grievance. "Cancel" culture become a real phrase, meant as a way to punish those who don't agree with the criminal thinking of so-called Social Justice Warriors. You step out of line on social media, and the Marxists will come for you and will cut you down.

Barack Obama opened the door to this sort of nonsense to become widespread, but he was only a match flicked onto a field already soaked in gasoline. And so, America burns, and would burn all the way down into the hellfire of Socialism, if it wasn't for the **Great American Patriot Donald J. Trump**.

You see, President Donald J. Trump comes from the old school. Born and raised in Queens and coming from New York, he doesn't mess around with this sort of nonsense. No sir, Patriot. He doesn't truck with BS. His Father, Fred C. Trump, put him in a military academy, not some Red Day Care Center like the ones littering every school district around the country. President Trump was raised right—in the old way and with the old American Values that made this country Number One in a world full of enemies and weak allies. President Donald J. Trump grew up wanting America to be more American, not more

Venezuelan.

President Trump recognized and has called out socialism since the day he announced his run for President of the United States. As a man who has built up his own brand to be recognized globally, he knows the **value** of Capitalism and the **rewards of hard work**. He has been around the world, closing deals left and right to build that brand. And he's seen up close what creeping socialism can do to the countries that fall for this crap.

Antifa, *****BLM**, the **Communist Party**—they are all part and parcel of a sick globalist movement designed to make us slaves for a sort of New World Order. They don't believe in God, or in borders, or in **Entrepreneurialism**. They believe in worshipping the State, that the Government is always here to help. (Hint: It isn't, it will never be, and can never be a "help.") President Trump doesn't buy that, and he won't let the American people buy it, either, because he knows just exactly how disastrous that belief is.

President Trump has always called out Antifa for what it is, has always called out the falsehoods of BLM, and tried to expose the sort of Marxist creeps that America was warned about in the 1950s. In fact, President Trump makes a consistent effort to keep it in the news cycle what these people are up to and to always shine a light on them and their preposterous actions. Though just like cockroaches, they scurry away the moment a light is shone upon them.

Sometimes they get away, but sometimes, President Trump manages to pinpoint who is who—and exactly what is what. And that's one of his greatest gifts as our Commander-in-Chief—Donald J. Trump keeps shining the light on them, keeps exposing them for what and who they really are.

When Facebook and Twitter start to ban conservatives— **President Trump calls them out**.

When BLM 'activists' pretend to be peaceful as a city burns— **President Trump calls them out**.

When Deceptive Democrat politicians and apologists continue to jabber and to talk from both sides of their mouth about Red China, the real source of the communist threat to our nation today—**President Trump calls them out**.

Being a leader is really about being able to communicate and articulate one's viewpoint and to rally others to his side. Make no mistake, Patriot, Donald J. Trump is doing just that. Even his enemies know exactly where he stands, and so do the good American Patriots, like you and me, who back up his cause.

Everyone knows what President Trump is talking about, and in fact, he is usually the conversation changer, making sure that the complicit MainStream Media (MSM) has to talk about things they don't want to talk about—like the bussed in protesters, the Soros funding, the Chinese influence.

There's not enough room in this book to disclose

all the evidence that President Trump is aware of, but let us just say that many members of the Democrat leadership and Soros and Big Tech will be fighting for the top bunk in prison soon. **Count on that, Patriot**.

These people, either the protesters in the street or the politicos in the backrooms, all have the same agenda of Communism—a worldwide conspiracy, based in Beijing and promoted by the U.N.

The Communists want to turn our schools into indoctrination camps, and our churches into blazing campfires.

They want all of our businesses to be run by the government, and run like the DMV.

They want us to kiss the backside of Mexico, and to let Canada be out front.

There's not a fake refugee they don't love, and there's not a real American they don't hate.

They want a mythological world that cannot exist without pain, and they are the biggest hypocrites in the world.

The celebrities and sports players who subscribe to this twisted belief system, how many of them are sharing the wealth? **NONE**. And they never will —they have all their money, just like George Soros, in Cayman Islands bank accounts, not paying a dime of the taxes they would raise on normal folks who don't have that sort of access to offshore banking. Same thing with the protesters as well—they aren't going to be paying a dime in taxes, they're going to be taking in millions in tax money for whatever welfare scheme they attached themselves to, or make work job, or an art degree that is useless but somehow society's fault they can't make it when grim reality sets in.

Donald Trump is at least honest. He doesn't want to be paying taxes either—and for good reason. Most of it is a waste, and most of it goes right down the drain and depletes vital resources from our businesses and communities; resources which are intended to be the means for them to thrive. A communist doesn't understand that because all they have in their minds is 60s era nonsense about "The Man" (read: White Man) putting them down and that every business out there is run by crooks. If that were the case, it would beg the question: how did America become so strong economically if it was run by crooks? No, the American system was run by men like Donald Trump—straight shooting businessmen. The wealth trickled down, and it worked for years.

President Trump is absolutely behind this, our American system, and wants to ensure it continues. He's not going to let the country go the way of the West Coast and Portland—look what he did there, authorizing federal agents to take out the trash. He made sure that the lawbreakers face the law. What a novel and unique concept!

President Trump has no time for niceties and the sort of diplomatic language previous Presidents have used (previous Presidents who sold our country down the river to the Chinese, the ultimate Marxist threat).

President Trump is here to keep our country safe and secure for American Business. He doesn't have time to have a beer summit with a Molotov cocktail throwing punk. He wants them jailed as they should be. Any person with a Molotov cocktail is an attempted murderer. I'm sure President Trump would use more aggressive measures if he could. But as you know Washington, they can't stand a take charge type of leader and will hamstring President Trump every step of the way and with any means necessary. With friends like these, who needs enemies?

The threat to America from the trained Communist elements like BLM and Antifa is as bad as it was during the Cold War and perhaps worse because the threat is coming from inside our very borders. These are people who are supposedly educated, who are so in love with the belief that they are doing the right thing, and that somehow in their own twisted imagination believe they are on the right side of history. **But how wrong they are!**

The Founding Fathers knew of the dangers of the

mob and that's why a Constitution was enshrined. But a Constitution is just a piece of paper really in the end; it takes men to enforce it. Donald J. Trump is our constitutional enforcer. Whatever Comey, the Clintons, BLM, Hussein Obama, Antifa, or whatever red diaper babies say, they are scared to be dealing with someone who might as well be another Founding Father by his attitude, diligence, and grace under pressure.

The central pillar of our support for President Donald J. Trump is that he will stand up to the communists in this country. And we will stand up for President Donald J. Trump. Will you stand up for our President, too, Patriot? We KNOW you will!

But there is one "Marxist" group that hasn't had much mention that should be called out. The Chinese Communists.

The ChiComs, as they are known in intelligence circles, or Chinese Communists, are also working to take America down a peg because they want to the boss of the planet. Despite acknowledging the failure of their own socialism and practicing capitalism better than any sort, they are spreading their tentacles of manipulation and greed from sea to shining sea.

What is there goal? In actuality, unlike the BLM

thugs or the Communists in Antifa, their goal is not some sort of revolution of the people over the rich, a re-do of the French Revolution. Look at China itself —home to more millionaires and billionaires than the U.S. itself could produce. Communism for them is just a term to dupe the liberals here in America into thinking they are on their side. It's a fact that they don't believe it anymore. Any Apple factory worker in the mainland can tell you that right away —communism, as a belief, is dead in China. But the Communist Party bosses still talk as if they believe in it, and still use it against the West in order to weaken us and open us up to economic conquest and political division.

No, the goal of the ChiComs is **WORLD DOM-INATION**. They want the world under the Chinese boot, and by accident or by purpose, started this policy of conquest once the Wuhan Virus was unleashed. They want President Xi to be the Emperor of the World. By cleverly manipulating Democrat politicians and college professors who love their oh so clever international programs, they are worming their way into the American system and turning it against itself.

The ChiComs are not stupid. Anyone who has had any dealing with that country when it comes to diplomacy realizes that from day one. They have a master game plan.

1. The first part of the plan is to suck up our

    intellectual property.

2. The second part is to suck up our extra cash and maintain an unfair trade advantage to keep up the money flow to Beijing.
3. The third part is to continue to manipulating these politicians we were dumb enough to keep in office.

When talking about politicians being dupes of the ChiComs, we mean both parties. Republican, Democrat—it doesn't matter. They were all falling for Chinese tricks. The only person who said otherwise? The only person that actually decided to finally strike back? President Donald J. Trump. Not Bush, not Clinton, and (without trying to laugh out loud) definitely not Hussein Obama.

No, President Trump called them on it. Just like he called them on the Chinese Virus that they brought into the world. These groups of Communists are perhaps the worst of the worst because they don't believe their own propaganda. They are heartless, cynical manipulators and as nationalist as the Nazis were. And like the Nazis, let us remember that few politicians in the west were ready to stand up to Hitler and his crew except for one man—Winston Churchill.

People will say that it's over the top to compare President Trump to Churchill, but we would say it's diminishing Trump by NOT comparing him to Churchill.

Trump has had to stand up to an enemy who is buying our allies, shaking down Africa, using our technology, and has a nuclear arsenal sitting around with the ability to point their weapons at every single one of our major cities. And he's been saying for years that we need to stand up to the People's Republic of China. But like Churchill for so long, he's been alone on this.

Well, no longer, Patriot! We are here and we are backing him up—remember the phrase "Against all enemies, foreign and domestic?" Well the ChiComs and the BLMs are the enemy, and we are damn sure ready to stand up to them with Donald J. Trump. President Trump figured out a long time ago who the real enemies were, and just as a Lincoln or a Washington, he's leading from the front ready to put these monsters down.

But he needs our help. Let's never forget that. Washington and Lincoln had the Army—let's make sure President Trump has the same. Even if you're not in the army, make sure you're in President Trump's corner, ready to fight for him and the American ideals he stands so firmly and proudly for.

The time is now, more than ever, for all hands on deck. The future is ours to keep, so let us follow the leadership, pluck, determination, and skill of Donald J. Trump. That's unless you want your children to grow up in a Cuban-style America trying to learn how to say "You want fries with that?" in Mandarin.

We know you don't want that, Patriot, and neither do we.

*** We feel the need to add a short statement here with regards to the BLM movement. It's particularly hurtful for us to see these radicals trashing our cities when President Trump has done so much to provide aid and assistance to Black Americans all across the spectrum, including advocating for proper policing reforms prior to many of the incendiary events that have taken place in the last few years. President Trump made it a mission to ensure Black Americans are treated fairly and with dignity, and these SJWs and protesters have essentially spit in his eye. It really is unfair and uncalled for.

We acknowledge that not all Black Americans are radicals and that many are fine Patriots who stand up and support President Trump. We thank them for that and encourage them to keep the faith and continue to support our President.

CLEANING UP THE MESS: PRESIDENT TRUMP VS IRAN AND NORTH KOREA

Let's go back in time a few years. George W. Bush came out with his "Axis of Evil," adroitly labeling three specific countries as being the biggest financial backers of terrorism and terrorist organizations on the planet. One was Iraq (no longer, thanks to Bush), one was Iran, and one was North Korea. Hostage taking Iran and Nuclear North Korea were always considered threats, and while let's be honest, Bush didn't do a good job with them, Obama basically decided to give away the cake away to a couple of third world bullies in order to get himself a second chance at that meaningless Nobel Prize that might as well be handed out of a cereal box.

They were basically coddled, cajoled, apologized for, and bribed for their good "behavior" and really thought the U.S.A. was just a weakened mess (which, truth be told, under Obama, was 100 percent God's Honest Truth.)

They were practically given the keys to the Oval Office and allowed to take a number two on the Resolute Desk. They were given billions of dollars in aid or in straight up suitcases of cash. For two countries that have terrorized their neighbors and who have killed innocent after innocent, you would have thought that these two were Hussein Obama's best friends after his second term.

They were laughing at us, big time. We know firsthand how many soldiers thought their personal sacrifices were in vain thanks to Obama's helpless attitude.

Obama gifted the Iranian regime $150 billion dollars that allowed them to regroup and expand their awful operations. $150 billon dollars to maim and murder innocent people.

There would be no way to undo Obama's damage which could be more consequential than we know (just as the Clintons' coddling of Bin Laden turned out to be more devastating in the long term), but President Trump made sure to put a stop to this sort of nonsense in a hurry.

The first thing was to ignore the appeasement deal towards Tehran. President Trump made sure to flush that agreement down the toilet, where it belonged. The Iranians are now facing hyperinflation, a stagnant economy, civil unrest, and the potential end of their sick Islamic revolution. President Trump is turning the screws on the Mullahs and we will soon see the Iranian people free and prosperous just as we saw the liberation of Eastern Europe under

President Reagan.

Iran has been boxed into a corner thanks to our President. Despite the naysaying by the MSM, John Kerry's inane ramblings, and Obummer's holier than thou attitude, America finally has the upper hand against the regime of hostage takers.

Iran is on the ropes thanks to the beating given to it by President Trump who knows how to play the dark and dirty game of international politics and intrigue. He is our Napoleon and Bismarck wrapped into one, a historical figure that hasn't been seen in American politics since the 1940s.

America's enemies have only respected America because of strength and determination, not because of a good speech. It was the case during the World Wars, it was the case during the Cold War, and it's the case now during the War on Terror. It shouldn't have to be said, but a terrorist regime like Iran cannot be reasoned with. It has to be made to feel afraid.

Nowhere has the Regime been made to feel more afraid than the drone strike that killed Qasem Soleimani. Soleimani was the head of all Iranian terror operations. More than that, he was the spinal cord of the cold hearted regime. His goons and his spies kept the dark mass of Iranian politics under the spell of the clerics and he was considered as indispensable as a person's right hand. Feared throughout the Middle East as a mastermind that could bring death and destruction. With his small army of fanatics he was able to strike anywhere, anytime and for all intents and purposes could get away with it due to existing U.S. policy before President Trump came onto the scene.

Soleimani wasn't to be touched because it would be "too inflammatory." The cowards of the "Deep State," the tenured bureaucrats who have let the whole world go to hell in the last twenty years, were content to let Public Enemy No.1, who actually targeted not only Middle Easterners but U.S. soldiers as well, to rampage with impunity.

For the cowards who grew up in coddled households and were given scholarships to Harvard for gender studies, they only thought of how to appease such a Government and to keep them placated. At no time did they have a true plan to take out such a bully and to put this bastard in his place.

In fact, with that $150 billion given to the Regime, they might as well have bought him three new houses, a corvette, and an all access pass to Disney World..

Under President Trump, this nonsense was put to bed. Just like the killing of the ISIS leader Al-Baghdadi helped to knock out ISIS, President Trump knocked out Iran's terror operations in one quick stroke. Like Churchill recognizing that appeasement only increases aggression, President Trump knew the time had come to stand up to the bullies and he did so with a mighty American Fist.

Notice how in today's heartless media environment that is dedicated to whipping up the ignorant into hating the President, that we barely even talk about the fact that President Trump destroyed ISIS and killed their leader. The fact that we have to remind readers that **Donald J. Trump destroyed ISIS** shows the abysmal depths to which the Mainstream Media have fallen.

Instead of happily celebrating the destruction of ISIS and ensuring that President Trump goes down in the pantheon of great American heroes, we got to hear nonsense about Stormy Daniels and other non-stories—that garbage was his family's business and no one else's. Do you care honestly who President Trump sleeps with or doesn't sleep with? No, of course not, Patriot. You're not sitting around collecting government checks and reading **People** magazine.

President Trump showed true leadership by knocking out Iran's Terror King and put Iran on notice that at any time we can bury one of their top leaders.

Violence is the only thing that these monsters can understand. Violence is the only universal language when it comes to violent, repressive, backwards, and expansionist regimes. Growing up in New

York City, back when it was basically a wasteland before Giuliani cleaned it up probably formed this correct worldview of President Trump.

When you are in a place that is dominated by gangsters and a permanent criminal class, anyone with a room temperature I.Q. or above can figure out real quickly how to deal with a bully—if they have the right sort of moral character. A stellar I.Q. and a functional spinal cord are what separates our President Trump from the rest of the American political establishment.

Soleimani was a single inkling of how tough President Donald J. Trump can be. Let's go back a few years. Kim Jong Un was rattling his pathetic saber and was threatening South Korea, Japan, and the U.S.A. North Korea has multiple nuclear weapons and one of the strongest militaries in the world. Despite having impoverished themselves with years of Marxist government and the Kim family's plundering, they can muster up enough military firepower to inflict serious lasting harm the innocents of Asia.

Kim was acting up because he didn't really know who our President is. Kim was under the impression that he was dealing with a Bill Clinton or an Oblivious Obama. He had no idea the sort of person President Trump is. He tested him.

Trump promised Kim that if he crossed the line, he would be met with "fire and fury" the likes of which the world had never seen. Kim took him at his word because he quickly got up to speed on Trump's character and understood that this was no ordinary President handpicked by the Deep State to continue a pattern of retreat and withdrawal.

Kim smartened up in a right hurry, and we saw something happen that no other President has ever been able to do—President Donald J. Trump sat down and talked peace with the head of North Korea.

North Korea has been in a state of war with the U.S. since the Korean conflict of the fifties and technically we have never been at peace with them. But now we are meeting with them in peace talks. No President, not even Eisenhower or Kennedy, could pull off such a perfect diplomatic coup.

President Trump is the one that made sure that Kim knew not to screw around anymore. Like an old school teacher from the 1950s, he put Kim in a dunce cap and made him sit in the corner. He didn't talk with Kim about his feelings, or whatever possible grudges the North Korean people had from a war that happened decades ago, he just made sure that Kim sat down and shut up.

And Kim did—in Singapore, Kim looked as if he was receiving a stern lecture from a beloved father figure. Kim settled down and the Korean peninsula is in a peaceful and secure state in a way that not even

George W. Bush could have imagined all those years ago when he mentioned the regime in his State of the Union address.

Imagine Barack Hussein Obama pulling off such a move! Not even your—or the Beltway Bumbler's—wildest fever dreams could see such an amazing diplomatic maneuver achieved with such an immense pay off.

And as of this printing, President Trump has also managed to normalize relations between U.A.E. and Bahrain with Israel. Yet another stroke of genius, and further proof that America—and the rest of the world—**NEED** Donald J. Trump to be reelected to a second term and beyond.

AGAINST THE SWAMP: PRESIDENT TRUMP VS THE DEEP STATE

It's no secret that Donald Trump is not, nor has ever been a bureaucrat of the Washington Machine/Swamp. He's never held office before. He's never been a Governor or a Senator, neither a councilman nor an alderman. He's been like 99% of our citizenry—working in the private sector, trying to make an honest dollar, and paying his taxes. He wasn't fresh out of Harvard, Yale, or some other Eastern Establishment school and straight into an internship with Henry Kissinger—he was actually working for a living and being, you know, more or less normal.

If you're not familiar with the way our system works, it should be known that the elite families of the East Coast produce spoiled sons and daughters who fill up the rank and file of our government. There's no real conspiracy here other than general nepotism and cronyism that infects all the appointed positions of Government.

It's a tale as old as the crucifixion—a grouping of elite families, with long held incestuous ties to each other, who are propping each other up. A paid internship here, an Ambassadorship there, an appointment over yonder—whatever happens, the elite of this country are self-perpetuating and making sure that they can feather their own nests and help advance the careers of their off-spring. There is no such thing as a meritocracy or advancement of the most knowledgeable—it's regrettably a system based on the advancement of the connected.

There's been so much of this for the last few decades that you have the blind leading the blind in a dangerous world of scheming characters. The U.S. Government is full of these types—self- assured, narcissistic, defensive, ignorant, and self-righteous.

They care nothing really for the United States but rather care more for the advancement of their families—think of Jesse Jackson's son, the latest Kennedy to come down the pipeline, Chelsea Clinton. A second cousin once removed to Jeb Bush. These characters infest every hall of government—from the CIA to the Department of Agriculture. They thrive on connections and cushy new jobs, and they think they know how to handle the rest of the world.

They never wanted a Donald Trump to come into town who didn't respect these old, unspoken agreements. Donald Trump comes from the private sector, where the phrase "You're Fired!" actually means something, not a temporary vacation where the same person who couldn't be trusted to produce a cup of coffee is switched to another important national position.

Donald Trump runs the Government like he runs his businesses—with an eye towards the bottom line. Yes, there has been a lot of turnover in his Administration. You'll see every empty talking head on almost every news network harping about the fact that X has been replaced by Y, and that there some sort of "shake up" in the administration.

Let's be honest here. If you were trying to get the best performing government since the Second World War, you wouldn't be settling for second best. You would only be allowing the best sort of characters into your orbit and ensuring that the Government has the best sort of people in all of the positions at all times. You wouldn't settle at all— and that's what President Trump is doing. **NOT SETTLING FOR SECOND BEST.** If you're not up to the task, it doesn't matter to him if you have had a long-term relationship with him before, or if you have helped him out during an election campaign. He demands results—just like the private sector. What a concept!

President Trump is most like Abraham Lincoln in this way. If you go back in your history, Abraham Lincoln had to go through General after General. The Civil War was raging, the Confederates were winning, and the country was crumbling. Like the Liberals of today, the rebels were winning (at least for a while) and changing the whole nation into

something worse and degrading the national character. Lincoln was never a battlefield commander, but
he knew—and his strength absolutely was this—he
knew how to pick out the right people for the job,
any personal feelings or attachments be damned.

With that sort of attitude (that this country can
only afford the best and can't ask for anything less
than that), Lincoln won the war. Donald Trump is
trying to win the war for the American people and
it's time for this sort of attitude, and President
Trump has embraced it.

President Trump has vanquished much of the
political class through expert strategy and thinking outside the box. Nasty Nancy Pelosi and Child-
ish Chuck Schumer have been outmaneuvered time
and again. How many times have they tried to take
down his Presidency? One almost loses count, but
of course there was the absolute embarrassment
of the Impeachment hearings that went absolutely
nowhere and accomplished nothing but the further
embarrassment of the political class who tried making a case out of libel and innuendo in order to take
down Donald J. Trump because he was the first President in decades to stand up to the global elite.

The Impeachment proceedings, "RussiaGate" or
whatever the Liberal traitors tried to lay on Donald
J. Trump's doorstep was the biggest exercise in political nonsense that has ever happened in Washington
D.C. There has been no proof of collusion, no proof of

any bad deeds whatsoever. The Washington Political Class can ramble all day and make up whatever cute stories they spit out to *The New York Times*, but nothing ever sticks.

Ask yourself the following question: if the Impeachment actually provided any proof of any wrongdoing by Donald J. Trump, do you not think that his Republican allies would have abandoned him in split second? The Deep State came up with a nonsensical dossier and pimped out page after page written in the comfort of Hillary Clinton's basement, probably on the same computer that she deleted all her emails from.

They came up with long term bureaucrats (the names are familiar, but shouldn't be mentioned in the same pages as our President) as false witnesses, they falsified records, and they pushed a media blitzkrieg that hasn't been seen in the history of the country.

Almost every talking head on almost every news channel was proclaiming the guilt of the President and the demise of his Administration. Almost every newspaper showing up on the doorsteps of American households were proclaiming the end of President Trump.

But President Trump prevailed, despite their machinations. His loyalists in the Senate, with the truth on their side and his articulate defense, snuffed out the would-be legislative coup that could have put a stop to the restoration of this country.

Think for a moment the incredible resources that the Deep State mustered against our President. They had mole after mole, useless bureaucrat after useless bureaucrat plugging up our Government like plaque plugging the arteries of a heart. There wasn't one corridor of the Government that President Trump could march down without having some Hillary hanger on, Clinton crony, or Obama opportunist screwing up his program.

Every newspaper that was connected with these creeps were putting out a mountain of lies every Monday. Every media group was spewing slander against his Administration. They finally pulled Nancy Pelosi, the Speaker of the House, into pushing these lies against him and triggering the process of impeachment.

But what happened in the end? Not a damn thing. Donald Trump successfully survived the biggest act of **Sedition** since Ethel and Julius Rosenberg gave away the secrets of our nuclear weapons to the Soviet Union. To be working in a world with enemies out there like Iran, North Korea, and China, and to have been handicapped the entire time by disloyal public servants who exhibited more loyalty to their patrons than to the people, and still be able to conduct any sort of policy whatsoever showcases the magnitude of the absolute greatness of President

Donald J. Trump.

WHAT IS TO BE DONE?
IN CONCLUSION

President Trump and the honest voters who have backed him up by either voting or by raising funds for his worthwhile cause have faced an onslaught of lies, media manipulation, international intrigue, and desperate conspiracies trying to derail the proverbial "Trump Train" and end one of the greatest, if not **the** greatest projects to restore the place, prestige, and light of the American people in a world full of darkness, bitterness, and inconsequential existence.

It truly has to be said that this is an odd crisis, brought forth only really because of the corruption that has slithered into and pervaded—and perverted—all levels of American life. This isn't a war with clear cut boundaries and known enemies, like the conflicts of old. Nor is it clearly a foreign conspiracy (though foreign elements such as the Chinese are a major part of it) like the heyday of the Soviets using foolish liberal intellectuals, money hungry traitors, and losers easily backed down with blackmail in order to be of use.

No, Patriot, this is a crisis brought forth by a disturbingly large portion of the American public who are focused on committing mass national suicide in a way that would make Jim Jones blush, a small but well-connected, influential and powerful Ultra-Socialist Cabal, and the Chinese to bend America into a New World Order.

Many (if not most) of these people involved in this conspiracy believe in the nonsense they are spewing. Some are opportunists, to be sure, who would proudly sell their own grandmother down the river for a few nickels (the Clintons come to mind—all of 'em), but most are brainwashed children produced by brainwashed adults who act like children.

You know the type, of course—the sort of people who put Obama posters in their studio apartments which are subsidized by the State, the slugs who sit outside your local grocery store waving petitions in your face in order to ban plastic straws, the loud ones with neon color hair who want to get a Professor banned because he said Che Guevara was a terrorist.

In a way, they are honest in their insanity, and in a way so naïve that one (for the briefest of moments) can almost forgive them for their nonsense. They would be harmless if it wasn't for the real brutes that pull their strings from the shadows. They would be just the sort of people that would ramble at you while you wait for your bus. You'd be on your way to work while they were on their way to pick up another student aid check, and you'd ignore them as best you could as if they were white static being emitted from a car radio.

The ultra-socialist cabal, on the other hand, is what pushes these creeps to be out in front of highways to block us so they can bitch and moan about whatever normal police procedure was used to subdue a crazed criminal. They own the media, dictating what the American people should be blasted with from their homes in the Hamptons or San Francisco. They sit down over conference calls and Skype sessions and look for whatever new issue they can find to rouse the Liberal left rabble and cause mayhem and sow seeds of discord. They do this on purpose. Do you really think America, the number one country in the world, is really such a terrible place?

Do you really think that police are just out to get minorities, that every company is full of environmentally destructive thugs, and that everyone is out to hurt each other? Hell no! Even with the amount of crime in this country, which is indeed ample and indeed a **REAL** issue, this isn't as bad as the Ultra-Socialist Cabal is painting it in their nightly news broadcasts, making you afraid of every little thing and making you wish that we had a new agency to deal with poverty and a new strange law enforcement arm to smash whatever the invisible threat is.

No, they are making sure that we feel afraid and

are begging for more Government. Unlike President Trump who trusts the institutions we have and the people serving them, they want to present a false issue (say police brutality) and push for some other growth of Government in order to take care of whatever nonsensical issue that was literally cooked up in George Soros' office space. They'll repeat whatever they've dreamed up in order to make us hate this country and to love our government.

Remember, there's always an agenda. Nobody is sitting in a newsroom ready to say, "Boy, this was a slow news day! Let's take a moment to talk about the good things that are going on."

No, the Ultra-Socialist Cabal needs us to be worked up constantly, with never a moment's peace of mind.

They want to weaponize our fears so that we can become part of some Global Community, some One World Order fantasy.

These people have been working on this for years. Remember, one of the last speeches John F. Kennedy gave was a warning to the American people about an insidious conspiracy.

THIS IS THE CONSPIRACY HE WAS WARNING US ABOUT.

We are seeing it happen, in real time, every single day, every single month.

The Crisis has to be solved by ensuring that at the very least that Donald Trump is maintained as our President for another term (and perhaps for another term beyond that). In our estimation, he really is the last best hope for continued freedom and prosperity in this country, if not in the world.

Voting for President Donald J. Trump is the best and easiest course of action to take to make sure that George Soros and his ilk don't appear on Mt. Rushmore, and that the Chinese anthem isn't heard every time Congress meets.

Voting for President Donald J. Trump ensures that the Cabal and the Criminals out there are put on notice, and that we keep having a Commander in Chief with guts, fortitude, and determination who will take the war to them.

Nobody, least of all us, Patriot, wanted to have to experience such events in their lifetime. For many of us, we grew up with, or at least heard of Ronald Reagan. He was a sweet and decent man, a person that almost any God-fearing American would love to have as their Grandfather, who over the course of two terms managed to bring back the country from the oblivion of Jimmy Carter's idiotic reign.

When Reagan retired in 1988 and was replaced by George Bush Sr., the Soviet Union, the arch-nemesis of humanity on par with Nazi Germany, had been destroyed. Eastern Europe was free. The World was seeing the end of the Communist experiment and globally, we were at peace. There was no terrorism, no Middle East horrors, no cop bashing.

For a brief period of time, the country was at its moral, economic, and political zenith. What a time it was to be alive! Sure, Bush Sr. in the end was no prize ("Read My Lips...) but we seemed to be on a sure trajectory. That is, until the Clintons, until Obama, until 9/11 of course.

We've lost our way. Voting is one thing, but we need to start a **New American Revolution** to really get this place going again. Trump winning re-election will be a delight, but it does not win us the war. We need foot soldiers to move through our local institutions, our state governments, all the way to D.C., and begin to kick out the swine that have been chewing up our tax dollars and feathering their nests for decades.

You have to find the right people. You need to get organized. You need to get militant. You can't be waiting for President Trump to do everything. Despite his nearly superhuman efforts to keep the Republic from sinking into the ash heap of history, he is only one man. A man, granted, that may indeed have divine help and who has been put into such an important position due to providence, but granted, he is just one man.

A President, despite what the Liberal Left wanted

you to think during the reign of Obama and his executive orders, is not a King and President Trump has to act with the utmost scruples within our Constitutional requirements.

But that doesn't mean we can't get up and mobilize for him and aid him in his quest to truly **Make America Great Again.**

We can stomp the swine out of office, we can push the protesters to the side, and we can stop buying Chinese products. Despite the ample propaganda that these companies from China are somehow privately owned (though you have to be a member of the Communist Party of China to make any real money), nothing is privately owned in China. It's a definite Marxist state. The Government owns you, not the people own the Government. So stop buying Chinese crap, stop voting for RINOs (Republicans in Name Only) and make sure that no Democrat ever gets elected or re-elected again!

We are in a desperate situation and steeped in an existential crisis that is profound, deep, and in many ways not just frightening, but absolutely terrifying.

And it's a situation where in some ways it's not obvious to every person who isn't tuned in to the political realm. Unlike a War with bombings left and right, and soldiers dying, it's a halfway silent crisis where for days nothing seems to happen to the average Joe. But it's a true crisis nonetheless, just as bad as any war.

But just like our **Great American Patriot Donald J. Trump**, we cannot be afraid. We have to look up to our President and be like him. We each and every one of us need to be as good an America as Donald J. Trump, and to many that might mean stepping out of our comfort zone.

Donald J. Trump, it should be reminded, left a cushy job, a billionaire lifestyle, and semi-retirement in order to fight for America. If he can do that for us, and suffer the libel, slander, and attacks of so many on all sides, then we can each do a little bit to actually back up such a strong, competent, and **necessary** President.

Please continue reading to find an amazing list of **Accomplishments made by President Donald J. Trump** during his Presidency thus far.

We acknowledge that because there are literally so many achievements by this administration that we may not have gotten them all down. We did our best to include the most important ones just so that anyone who isn't a supporter of the President can really get an unbiased, unvarnished look what he's been able to do for our country and the world. In time, we may revise the Accomplishments section to include President Trump's ever-growing list of successes for our country and for the American

People.

Patriot, we once again want to thank you for your support of this Manifesto and for your continued support of the Great American Patriot Donald J. Trump.

Please, do consider taking to heart our request that you share this book on ALL of your social media channels, being sure to tag President Trump, FLOTUS, Vice President Pence, Donald Jr., Ivanka, Jared, Eric, and anyone else you can so that perhaps President Trump will see this work and know that there are True Patriots in his corner, fighting for him and fighting for the United States of America.

God Bless You All, God Bless President Donald J. Trump, and God Bless America.

ACCOMPLISHMENTS OF THE UNITED STATES UNDER THE LEADERSHIP OF THE GREAT AMERICAN PATRIOT DONALD J. TRUMP

IMMIGRATION

As we've stated emphatically throughout this Manifesto, President Trump is tirelessly working to secure our borders against illegal immigration to keep us safe.

• President Trump continues to fulfill his promise to build a border wall, with large portions having already been finished or under construction. It's expected that 450 miles will be finished by the end of 2020.

• The Trump Administration has constructed no less than 100 miles of new border wall system to keep illegals out. In fact, the new wall has contributed to a 56% overall decrease in the number of illegal migrant arrivals at our southern border.

• Currently, 167 miles of wall is under construction in high entry border sectors such as San Diego and El Centro, California; El Paso, Texas; and Yuma, Arizona.

• Under President Trump, the U.S. Border Patrol has arrested and removed from society many hundreds of members of dangerous, violent, and deadly gangs.

• The President has strongly enforced our nation's immigration laws by cracking down on illegal immigration; he has taken aim at so-called "sanctuary cities" and brought them to heel.

• President Trump has strongly called on Congress to close dangerous loopholes in existing laws such as the ridiculous "Catch and Release" fiasco, bringing an end to chain migration, and ending the massive failure that is the visa lottery program which enables illegal immigration.

• The Administration is looking to end or severely curtail the *Flores Settlement Agreement* that requires the government to release families into the country after 20 days. This loophole has been exploited by vile smugglers who use innocent children as pawns to enter our country.

• We are closing asylum loopholes—recently, the Administration instituted a new rule requiring migrants who come to our border to have previously applied and been denied asylum to a country they passed through. This alone will curb legal and illegal immigration tremendously.

• The Trump Administration announced the enactment of a "Public Charge Rule" that will ensure non-citizens do not abuse our nation's public benefits. This rule went into effect on October 15th, 2019.

• President Trump was successful in his efforts to get Mexico and the Northern Triangle countries to step up and help stop the crisis at the border. President Trump's successful negotiations have led to 28% drop in migrants taken into custody.

• President Trump announced a new immigration proposal that would modernize our system and secure the border even better.

• The Administration has made it a top priority to end the evil practice of human trafficking and is using numerous resources to do so.

• The Administration provided funding to support the National Human Trafficking Hotline.

• The Anti-Trafficking Coordination Team (ACTeam) initiative more than doubled convictions of human traffickers and increased the number of defendants charged in ACTeam districts.

AMERICA'S FOREIGN POLICY

President Trump has restored our nation's standing in the world and is standing up to bad actors to protect our interests.

• The United States has successfully decimated ISIS under the leadership and guidance of President Donald J. Trump.

• Under President Trump, the number one terrorist leader Abu Bakr al-Baghdadi was eliminated, ensuring he can no longer harm Americans abroad or at home.

• President Trump ordered the killing of Qassem Soleimani, the head of Iran's elite Quds Force, an evil, ruthless, and deadly terrorist responsible for countless deaths.

• President Trump fulfilled his promise to name Jerusalem Israel's capital city and moved the U.S. Embassy there.

• President Trump held two historic summits with North Korean leader Kim Jong Un, further demonstrating the Administration's commitment to a denuclearized Korean peninsula.

• President Trump withdrew the U.S. from the disastrous Iran Nuclear Agreement and instituted the toughest sanctions in history to drive the regime's oil exports to zero.

• In June 2019, President Trump signed an executive order that authorized expanded sanctions against Iran.

• The Administration has vigorously and quickly enforced red lines against regimes and individuals that use or have been known to use chemical weapons.

• The Trump Administration imposed hard-hitting sanctions against Iran's national bank.

AMERICAN JUDICIAL ACHIEVEMENTS

President Trump continues to reshape the Federal judiciary at a record pace and is following through on his promise to appoint judges who will uphold the Constitution and rule of law.

• President Trump continues to reshape the Federal judiciary at a record pace.

• President Trump has installed more federal court judges than any president in the past four decades.

• The President is following through on his promise to appoint judges who will uphold the Constitution and rule of law for generations to come.

• President Trump has nominated, and the Senate has confirmed a grand total of 187 Article III judges.

• 2 Supreme Court Justices – Justice Gorsuch and Justice Kavanaugh.

• 50 Circuit Court judges.

• 133 District Court judges.

• 2 Court of International Trade Judges

• President Trump's judicial confirmations have "flipped" 3 – 2nd, 3rd, 11th Circuits - federal appeals courts to Republican.

• In 2018, President Trump broke the record for the most circuit court of appeals judges (29) confirmed in the first 2 years of a presidency.

• President Trump has vowed fill the vacant seat left on the Supreme Court bench left by the passing of Justice Ruth Bader Ginsburg, citing the Constitutional responsibility of the Administration to fill the vacancy as expediently as possible.

Health Care

President Trump has reduced the cost of health care by repealing Obamacare and giving American Families a choice again, and he has taken significant steps to fight the appalling opioid epidemic.

• President Trump has prioritized fixing our broken health care system and worked with Congress to implement a system that works for all Americans.

• The President has made it clear patients with preexisting conditions will be protected, no exceptions.

• The unfair individual mandate penalty imposed by the disastrous Obamacare debacle has been eliminated.

• Association Health Plans have been expanded.

• Short-term, limited duration insurance plans have been extended.

• President Trump is working to implement his plan to lower prescription drugs.

• Under the Trump Administration, the nation has seen the first ever decline of average benchmark premiums on the federal health care exchange.

• The President signed an Executive Order to improve seniors' health care and improve the overall fiscal sustainability of the Medicare program.

• Reforms to expand Medicare Advantage options and Health Reimbursement Accounts have been updated and expanded.

• President Trump mobilized his entire Administration to address the drug addiction and opioid abuse crises by declaring a Nationwide Public Health Emergency.

• President Trump signed the SUPPORT for Patients and Communities Act to fight the crippling opioid epidemic.

• The Trump Administration launched FindTreatment.gov, a public resource to help combat substance abuse in all forms.

• President Trump signed an Executive Order that increases medication price and quality transparency.

• The Administration has committed to putting an end to surprise billing.

• HHS is finalizing a mandate that will require hospitals to make prices publicly available online and in a more consumer-friendly format.

• The Administration has proposed a rule to require

insurance companies and group health plans to provide enrollees with cost estimates upfront.

• The Trump Administration has promoted innovation and solutions to expand treatment options for Americans living with disease, including HIV/AIDS, kidney disease, pediatric cancer, Alzheimer's, and many more.

• The Administration launched a program to provide the HIV prevention drug PrEP to uninsured and patients for zero cost.

• Signed the bipartisan Tobacco-Free Youth Act to raise the nationwide age for purchasing tobacco and vaping products to 21 years old.

• Costly Obamacare taxes were repealed, including the "Cadillac tax" and the Medical Device Tax.

THE AMERICAN ECONOMY

President Donald J. Trump's policies have kicked the American Economy into overdrive, despite all the obstacles he's faced.

• Since President Trump was elected 7.3 million jobs have been created.

• In 2019, 2.1 million new jobs were created.

• In 2019, 1.5 million jobs were added for women. This accounts for more than 50% of total job gains for the first time ever.

• Over 500,000 manufacturing jobs have been created since the President was elected.

• Highlights of December 2019 jobs report: 174,000 jobs were created in December.

• December marked the 22nd consecutive month that the unemployment rate had been at or below 4%.

• For 22 consecutive months, wage growth was near or above 3%.

• Throughout the Trump Administration we have seen record low unemployment for women, African

Americans, Latino Americans, and Asian Americans.

• The Hispanic American unemployment rate remained at a near record low of 4.2%.

• The Asian American unemployment rate was 2.5%, near a historic low.

• The adult women's unemployment rate hit 3.2%, the lowest since 1953.

• The Dow Jones Industrial Average hit record highs more than 100 times so far under President Trump.

• Under President Trump, 7 million people have come off of the food stamp program.

• Under President Trump's leadership, Congress has passed historic tax cuts and relief for hard-working Americans. The Tax Cuts and Jobs Act is the first major tax reform signed in 30 years.

• As a result of the historic tax cuts, nearly 9,000 Opportunity Zones were created in all 50 states, DC, and 5 territories. Opportunity Zones will spur $100 billion in private capital investment and impact nearly 35 million Americans.

• The Tax Cuts and Jobs Act increased the Child Tax Credit by 100% keeping more money in the pockets of hardworking mothers.

• Economic confidence rebounded to record highs under President Trump because his pro-growth policies have and continue to put American workers and businesses first.

• President Trump has rolled back unnecessary job-killing regulations at a historic pace, and continues to do so.

• The Trump Administration has cut eight and a half regulations for every new rule.

▪ This far exceeds the promise made to cut 2 regulations for every 1 regulation added.

• Regulatory costs have been slashed by nearly $50 billion and will have saved taxpayers $220 billion once actions are implemented.

• The deregulation efforts will save American households an estimated $3,100 each per year on average.

• The Administration formed the Governors' Initiative on Regulatory Innovation which aims to better align state and Federal efforts to cut additional unnecessary regulations and costs.

AMERICAN FREE TRADE

President Trump continues to deliver on his campaign promise to correct lopsided trade imbalances throughout all of the United States' business concerns.

• The Trump Administration has taken unprecedented steps to modernize and improve trading practices and negotiate freer, fairer, and reciprocal trade agreements with our global allies.

• President Trump kept his promise to deliver a modern and rebalanced trade deal to replace NAFTA. The United States-Mexico-Canada Agreement (USMCA)

• The USCMA will spur economic growth, create 176,000 jobs, add an estimated $68.2 billion to the U.S. economy, and raise wages.

• President Trump negotiated a new United States-Japan trade deal with Prime Minister Shinzo Abe. Japan is one of our strongest economic partners and this trade deal builds on that partnership. It is a huge win for American farmers, ranchers, workers, and businesses.

• The Administration revised the United States-Korea Free Trade Agreement (KORUS) to make it more beneficial to American workers.

• The President and European Union President Juncker agreed to a new trade deal that strengthens and reforms our trade relationship. The agreement:

• Works toward zero tariffs, zero non-tariff barriers, and zero subsidies on non-automotive industrial goods.

• Makes it easier for the EU to purchase liquefied gas.

• Reduces trade and bureaucratic obstacles between the U.S. and the EU.

• Addresses unfair trade practices.

• President Trump agreed to a phase one trade deal with China that includes an extremely strong enforcement mechanism.

• President Trump withdrew the United States from the fundamentally flawed Trans-Pacific Partnership.

• President Trump has forced our allies to recommit to NATO.

• The Trump Administration has protected farmers from unfair trade practices by authorizing $12 billion in aid to the American agricultural heartland under The Commodity Credit Corporation Charter Act.

THE ENVIRONMENT

President Trump is continually promoting a clean and healthy environment from sea to sea for all Americans.

• The President and the Administration are continuing to pursue policies that encourage environmental protection while promoting economic growth.

• Since 2005, US energy related carbon emissions have declined more than any other country in the world. This is expected to further decrease in 2020 and beyond.

• Our nation's environmental record is one of the strongest in the world. According to the White House, from 1970 to 2018, the combined emissions of the most common air pollutants fell 74% while the economy grew over 275%.

• We have the cleanest air on record and remain a global leader for access to clean drinking water. The President has taken important steps to restore, preserve, and protect our land, air, and waters.

• The Save our Seas Act was signed into law in 2018. This law reauthorized the NOAA Marine Debris Program, promoting international action to reduce marine debris and authorizing cleanup and response actions as may be needed.

• The EPA has taken significant steps to clean up our contaminated sites and hazardous sites.

• In FY2018, the EPA completed cleanup work on 22 Superfund sites from the National Priorities list. This is the largest number in one year since 2005.

• The EPA is more efficiently implementing air quality standards that will better protect the environment and human health, not only in America, but around the globe.

• President Trump signed legislation designating 1.3 million new acres of wilderness—the largest public lands legislation in a decade.

• The Department of the Interior proposed to open more than 1 million acres of land for expanded hunting and fishing access to Americans.

• The President took important action to improve management of forests to help prevent devastating forest fires.

• The President's management of our nation's lands is fair and balanced and promotes conservation while encouraging good stewardship and expanding recreational opportunities.

• President Trump issued changes to the National Environmental Policy Act (NEPA) to reduce regulation and allow for vital infrastructure and transportation projects to move forward without unnecessary delays.

AMERICAN ENERGY

President Trump's policies have begun to unleash our nation's vast and underrated energy potential.

• President Trump signed an Executive Order to expand offshore oil and gas drilling and open more leases to develop offshore drilling, a stable and vital source of American energy potential.

• The Administration acted aggressively to increase exports of energy resources to the global market and allowed immediate financing for coal and fossil energy projects.

• President Trump has approved the infrastructure and provided the resources needed to unleash Oil and Gas production in the U.S.

• The Keystone XL and Dakota Access pipelines were approved, supporting an estimated total of 42,000 jobs and $2 billion in wages.

• The New Burgos Pipeline, a cross-border project that will export U.S. gasoline to Mexico, was approved.

• The Trump Administration reversed President Obama's moratorium on new leases for oil and gas development on Federal lands.

• The President rescinded President Obama's costly and burdensome Clean Power Plan.

• The President proposed the Affordable Clean Energy Rule to reduce greenhouse gasses, empower states, promote energy independence, and facilitate economic growth and job creation throughout the United States.

• The Administration has rescinded many costly Obama-Era regulations, including the methane emissions rule which would have cost American energy developers an estimated $530 million annually.

• The President announced his intent to withdrawal the U.S. from the unfair Paris Climate Accord and followed through.

AMERICAN AGRICULTURE

President Trump and his Administration continue to help one of our Nation's most valuable assets: Our Farmers.

• In 2018, President Trump signed a sweeping new Farm Bill into law.

• The Farm Bill provides support and stability to our farmers, expands crop insurance, doubles the amount farmers can borrow, and helps open new markets for our farmers.

• The President authorized the year-round sale of E15 gasoline which provided a boost to America's corn growing communities.

• Red tape restrictions that have hamstrung and harmed American farmers have been rolled back. This includes eliminating the burdensome Obama-era Waters of the United States rule.

• The historic Tax Cuts and Jobs Act protects family farmers from the estate tax.

• Thanks to the President's historic tax cuts legislation, the effective tax rate for farmers is expected to fall from 17.2% to 13.9%.

• President Trump is standing up for America's farmers by negotiating fairer, freer, and more reciprocal trade deals that remove barriers and open markets for American farmers.

• President Trump negotiated the United States-Mexico-Canada Agreement (USMCA), getting a better deal for American farmers and ranchers. • The USMCA will increase America's Agricultural exports by $2.2 billion.

▪ The USMCA will eliminate Canada's discriminatory programs that allow low-priced dairy products to undersell our nation's dairy producers.

▪ USMCA includes expanded market access for dairy products, eggs, and poultry.

• In a deal with the European Union, American soybean exports will be increased dramatically.

• President Trump reached a new trade agreement with Japan. As a result, Japan will eliminate or reduce tariffs on approximately $7.2 billion in U.S. agricultural exports.

• President Trump continues to stand up to China and their unfair trade practices which target our farmers. The Administration provided $16 billion in funds to support our farmers against unfair trade retaliation.

• The Trump Administration continue to support

and expand markets for America's farmers.

• Japan's market has been opened to all American beef.

• Restrictions have been eliminated on:

• American pork exports to Argentina.

• American beef to Brazil.

• Idaho chipping potatoes to Japan.

• American poultry to South Korea.

• President Trump signed an Executive Order directing Federal agencies to streamline the agricultural biotechnology regulatory process.

• The Trump Administration is working to promote connectivity in Rural America by investing in rural broadband internet services, thereby granting more internet access to those in need.

• President Trump is working to protect our National Forests.

• In 2018, the President signed an Executive Order aimed at increasing responsible forest management and coordinating Federal, State, Tribal, and Local assets to prevent and combat wildfires.

• In order to preserve the health of our forests, the Agriculture Improvement Act of 2018 was signed into law.

• President Trump and his Administration continue to provide necessary disaster relief to impacted areas.

AMERICAN EDUCATION

President Trump and his administration are focused on putting students and families first.

• The President understands the importance of education and continues to declare the last week in January National School Choice Week.

• The President signed an historic Executive Order that promotes and protects free speech on college campuses.

• President Trump and his Administration support the Education Freedom Scholarships and Opportunity Act.

• In 2019, President Trump signed a memorandum that eliminates 100% of student loan debt for permanently disabled veterans; further proof of his support for our veterans, too.

• The President continues to work with the Department of Education to expand transparency and give students expanded access to vital information about the potential career outcomes of the programs they enroll in.

• President Trump has made Historically Black Colleges and Universities a priority, including appropriating more money to HBCUs in one year than any other president in history, and establishing a Presidential Board of Advisors on HBCUs.

• President Trump signed the FUTURE Act into law. The law permanently funds HBCUs and simplifies the FAFSA application process.

• The President is committed to expanding and strengthening education in science, technology, engineering, and mathematics (STEM) programs.

• President Trump issued a Presidential Memorandum encouraging the Department of Education to promote STEM, especially Computer Science.

• President Trump directed more than $200 million per year to technology education grants for women and programs that encourage participation in STEM careers.

• The President signed the bipartisan reauthorization of the Carl D. Perkins Career and Technical Education Act. This law provides necessary training for students and workers to succeed in the 21st century economy.

• The President donated his 2017 second quarter salary to the Department of Education. The funds were used to host a STEM focused camp for students.

• President Trump signed the INSPIRE Act which encourages NASA to reach more women and girls in order that they may participate in STEM programs and pursue careers in aerospace.

• The President signed an Executive Order to expand apprenticeships across all major aspects of industry in America.

• President Trump has strongly encouraged state and federal lawmakers to expand school choice.

• The Administration lowered regulatory hurdles and restored flexibility to schools with respect to menus in their cafeterias.

• President Trump is committed to making our schools safer.

• President Trump encouraged passage of the STOP School Violence Act to provide funding grants to schools to improve security measures.

• The Administration established a Commission on School Safety to examine ways to make schools safer for all students and teachers.

• Additionally, the Administration proposed a new $5 billion annual tax credit to promote school choice. This move is supported by 2/3rds of Black Americans.

THE UNITED STATES MILITARY AND OUR HONORED VETERANS

President Trump is protecting America and our Allies by rebuilding our Military and ensuring our Veterans receive the care they deserve.

• President Trump has restored American military strength and might.

• Under President Trump's leadership, Congress passed three historic National Defense Authorization Acts (NDAA).

• The FY2020 NDAA includes a much needed 3.1% pay raise for our troops at every rank.

• The FY2020 NDAA establishes the United States Space Force to ensure American dominance in space.

• President Trump signed the Veterans Accountability and Whistleblower Protection Act to allow senior officials in the Department of Veterans Affairs (V.A.) to fire failing employees and establish safeguards to protect whistleblowers.

• The President signed the V.A. Choice and Quality Employment Act of 2017 to authorize $2.1 billion in additional funds for the Veterans Choice Program (VCP).

• The Trump Administration created a new White House V.A. Hotline, staffed by Veterans and family members.

• The Administration has secured a record $8.6 billion in funding for mental health services with the goal of ending the tragic epidemic of Veteran suicide.

• The Trump Administration has created the PRE-VENTS initiative, a task force aimed at unifying the efforts of government, businesses, and nonprofit groups to help our veterans.

• The President has secured $73.1 billion for the Department of Veterans Affairs—the highest funding for the VA in history.

• Veterans Affairs increased transparency and accountability by launching an online "Access and Quality Tool." This provides veterans a way to access wait time and quality of care data.

• In 2019, President Trump signed a memorandum that eliminates 100% of student loan debt for permanently disabled veterans.

• The President called upon all 50 states to ensure

that disabled Veterans do not pay state tax on their forgiven debts.

• The unemployment rate among Veterans is at a record low of 2.8%.

• 9.1 million veterans are employed.

• The number of unemployed Veterans has been reduced by 40% under President Trump.

• In November 2019, President Trump became the first president to walk in the New York City Veterans Day Parade.

AMERICAN WOMEN

Under President Trump's Administration, women have been empowered and provided with the necessary tools and resources to reach their full economic potential.

• Women have experienced record low unemployment under President Trump.

• Since he was elected, President Trump has created over 4.3 million new jobs for women.

• In 2019, 1.5 million jobs were added for women. This accounts for more than 50% of total job gains for the first time ever.

• In December, the adult women's unemployment rate hit 3.2%, the lowest since 1953.

• The unemployment rate among women has been under 4% for 18 straight months.

• During the President's first year in office, the number of American women in poverty fell by nearly 600,000.

• Thanks to the Tax Cuts and Jobs Act, the child tax credit was doubled to $2,000 per child.

• President Trump was the first president to include a paid family leave policy in 2 separate budget proposals.

• The FY 2020 NDAA included paid parental leave for federal workers.

• The President and his Administration are committed to keeping families and communities safe.

• The Trump Administration has prioritized empowering women to pursue careers and realize their economic potential.

• President Trump directed more than $200 million per year to technology education grants for women and programs that encourage participation in STEM careers.

• President Trump signed an Executive Order establishing the National Council For The American Worker.

• Over 300 companies and associations of all size and industry have signed the Administration's Pledge to America's Workers, promising to create more than 14 million education, training, and skill-building opportunities over the next 5 years.

• Ivanka Trump created the **Women's Global Development and Prosperity Initiative (W-GDP)** to help 50 million women in 22 developing countries realize their economic potential by 2025.

• Additional Trump Administration efforts to empower women globally include:

• **The Women Entrepreneurs Finance Initiative (We-Fi):** Aims to mobilize more than $2.6 billion in capital for women entrepreneurs in 26 developing countries.

• **The Women Connect Challenge:** Seeks to grow women's access to digital technology and bridge the digital gender divide.

• **The 2X Women's Initiative:** Aimed at mobilizing $1 billion in capital to support women living in the developing world. This initiative has already mobilized more than $140 million from the private sector to support women in Latin America and the Caribbean.

BLACK AMERICANS

Black Americans have a true friend and a fierce champion in President Trump.

• President Trump has created an astonishing 1.6 million new jobs for Black Americans since his election.

• In December 2019, the Black unemployment rate was at 5.9%.

• The Black American unemployment rate was at or below 7% for 23 consecutive months.

• Prior to President Trump's administration, the Black unemployment rate had never dipped below 7%.

• In 2019, the Black American unemployment rate hit a record low and remained below 7% for the entire year.

• Under President Trump, incomes for Black Americans have increased by 2.6%.

• Under the Trump Economy, wages are continuing to rise, which significantly benefits the lowest-paid workers.

• The poverty rate among Black Americans is at its lowest level in history.

• Under President Trump, 350,000 fewer Black Americans are living in poverty.

• During the President's first year in office, the Black American poverty rate fell to 21.2% down from 22% the year before.

• As a result of the historic Tax Cuts and Jobs Act, nearly 9,000 Opportunity Zones were created in all 50 states, DC, and 5 territories.

• Opportunity Zones will create jobs and spur investment in disadvantaged communities.

• These Opportunity Zones will spur $100 billion in private capital investment and impact 1.4 million minority households.

• President Trump signed the historic FIRST STEP Act into law.

• The FIRST STEP ACT has been widely hailed as the most meaningful criminal justice reform in a generation.

• This landmark legislation included necessary reforms to our justice system, improves our prison system, and prepares inmates for reentry into our communities so that they live meaningful lives with purpose.

• As a result of the First Step Act, more than 3,000 Americans have been released from prison and 90% of those who have had their sentences reduced are Black Americans.

• The First Step Act shortens mandatory minimum sentences for nonviolent drug crimes and provides judges greater liberty to bypass mandatory minimums, and instead issue sentences based on the circumstances of individual offenders.

• The law also allows offenders sentenced under racially motivated mandatory minimums to petition for their cases to be re-evaluated; a first in the history of the United States criminal justice system.

• President Trump was awarded the 2019 Bipartisan Justice award by the nonprofit 20/20 Bipartisan Justice Center. The President received this award for his "ability to work across the aisle to achieve meaningful progress in reforming our criminal justice system."

• President Donald J. Trump has committed his Administration to advancing second chance hiring for former prisoners. This includes launching a "Ready to Work Initiative."

• The Trump Administration has fought for a federal tax credit on donations that fund scholarships to private schools, a proposal supported by 64% of

Black Americans.

• President Trump has made supporting Historically Black Colleges and Universities (HBCUs) a top priority.

• In February 2017, President Trump announced the President's Board of Advisors on HBCUs.

• The President signed an Executive Order on HBCUs in February 2017, the earliest any President has signed an Order on HBCUs.

• The EO established an Interagency Working Group to advance and coordinate work regarding HBCUs.

• The federal HBCU initiative office was moved back into the White House, a move that leaders had requested under President Obama.

• President Trump has appropriated more money than any other president to HBCUs.

• The President signed legislation to increase federal funding for HBCUs by 13%, the highest level ever.

• President Trump signed the FUTURE Act into law. The law permanently funds HBCUs and simplifies the FAFSA application.

• The President worked with Congress to lift the ban on Pell Grants on summer classes.

• Through the Capital Financing Program, the Administration has provided more than $500 million in loans to HBCUs.

• The President directed the entire federal government to develop a strategy to support HBCUs. To date, this has been supported by 32 departments and agencies.

• The Administration has forgiven more than $300 million in outstanding debt for four schools impacted by natural disasters and the budget provided $10 million to defer loan payments for 6 school facing financial difficulties.

• The Department of Education worked with HBCUs to protect $80 million in Title III carryover funding.

• President Trump took a big step to end discriminatory restrictions to prevent faith based HBCUs from accessing federal support.

• The Administration continues to work with HBCUs to expand apprenticeship opportunities, career choices, and ensure they are receiving adequate support.

LATINO AMERICANS

Under President Trump's leadership and care, the Latino American community has thrived and excelled.

• Under President Trump, Latino Americans have experienced record low unemployment.

• More than 2.9 million jobs have been created for Latino Americans since the President was elected. o In December, the Latino American unemployment rate was at a near record low of 4.2%.

• The Hispanic American unemployment rate hit several record lows in 2019, including falling below 4% for the first time in history.

• The median Latino American income rose by $1,786 during President Trump's first year in office. o In 2017, the median Latino American income hit its highest ever recorded level ($50,486).

• Since taking office, the Latino American homeownership rose by more than a percentage point (46.3% to 47.4%).

• In addition to the booming economy, President Trump renegotiated freer and fairer trade deals such as the USMCA.

• President Trump has stood up to Socialism and Communism in Venezuela, Cuba, and Nicaragua.

• Thanks to pressure from President Trump, 50 countries followed President Trump's leadership in recognizing Juan Guaidó as the legitimate leader of Venezuela.

• The Trump administration has rolled back President Obama's disastrous rapprochement with Cuba, which only benefited the country's dictatorship instead of its people.

• At the direction of President Trump, the Treasury Department has imposed sanctions against senior officials in the Nicaraguan regime for their role in human rights abuses and undermining democracy.

• The President has made it clear that American interests do not align with failed socialist policies.

ASIAN AMERICANS

Under President Trump's leadership Asian American unemployment has reached record lows.

• In December, the Asian American unemployment rate was 2.5%, near a historic low.

• The lowest ever record unemployment rate for Asian Americans (2.1%) came in June 2019.

The authors and publishers would like to take one last opportunity to thank you, Patriot, for your support of our work and for your support of our President, Donald J. Trump. Share this work and your support of the President far and wide.

With your help, we will see that Donald J. Trump is reelected to the Presidency so that he may continue the important work that he has started in our country and for the world.

President Donald J. Trump has really and truly lived up to his promise to **MAKE AMERICA GREAT AGAIN.**

Don't forget to vote, Patriot. Don't let the Liberal Media frighten you or intimidate you into not letting your voices be heard loud and clear on Election Day.

You have the absolute RIGHT and sacred DUTY to cast your vote for President Donald J. Trump and Vice President Mike Pence.

If you don't vote for President Trump, you're voting for Anarchy, Violence, Communism, and all of the dangers, both internal and external, that threaten our Republic and our very Way of Life.

STAND UP, PATRIOTS, AND MAKE YOUR VOICES HEARD LOUD AND CLEAR. WE WANT PRESIDENT DONALD J. TRUMP FOR 4 MORE YEARS!

YOU CAN MAKE THAT HAPPEN, SO DO IT!!!